practice you

a journal

ELENA BROWER

SOUNDS TRUE
BOULDER, CO

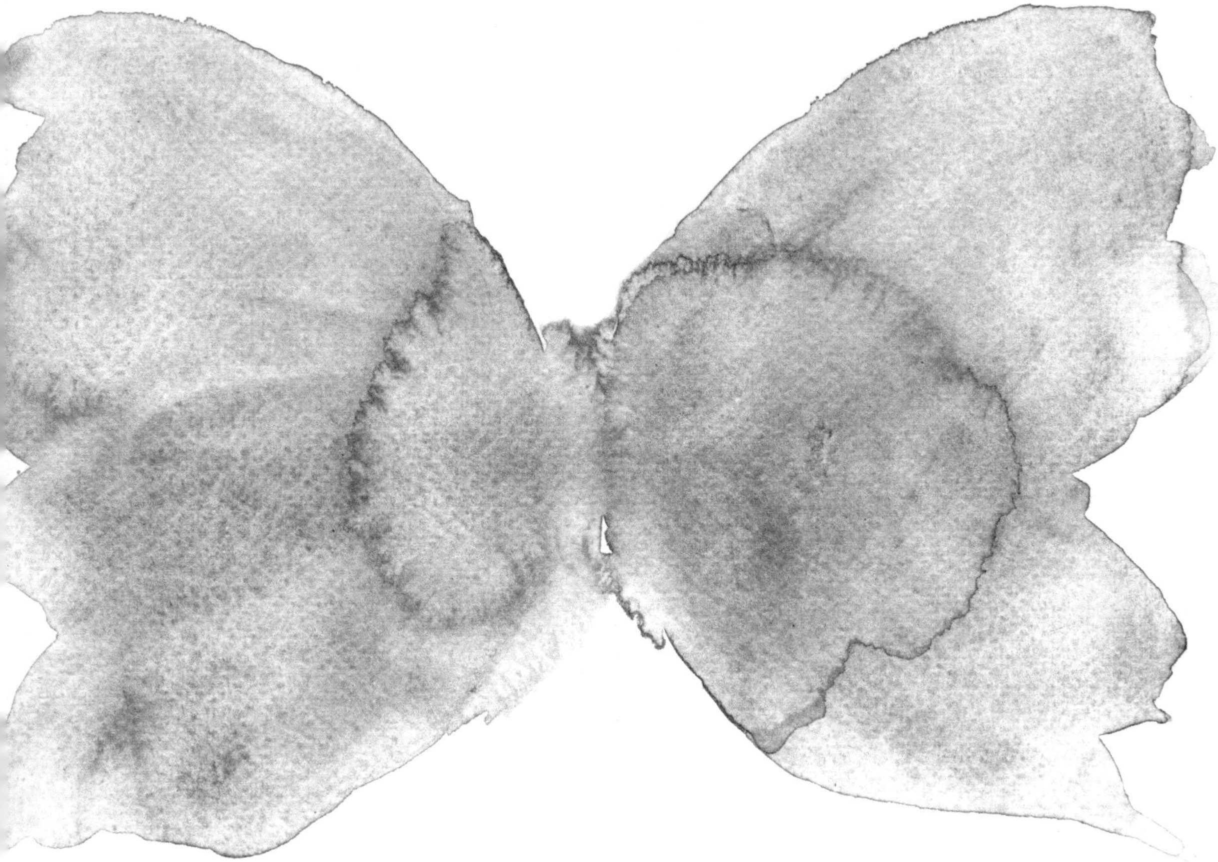

dedicated to my mama.

my attention is my prayer.

I AM. I FEEL. I DO.

my presence is my communication.

I LOVE. I SPEAK.

my intention is my projection.

I SEE. I UNDERSTAND.

my breathing
is my reflection.

I TRUST. I SERVE.

introduction

YOU'VE BEEN PRACTICING YOU your entire life. You have always been the author of your own experience. This book is an invitation to become the author of a sacred text of your own design, an opportunity to write a personal field guide to your highest self.

How can you practice your best self? Having endured times of doubt, disconnection, and insufficiency, I've learned that the only way out of that morass is to go inward. In self-observation, study, and reflection on the offerings of my teachers, my understanding continues to unfurl. When I turn to my own journals for the wisdom I need, I learn countless lessons from looking back on my own questions, then revisiting and refining the answers. Those two decades-worth of notebooks hold medicinal wisdom that reveals and heals negative assumptions, unearths forgotten resources, and provides essential reminders from within my own experience. The book you hold in your hands is meant to serve you with access to your own intelligence as you revise, revisit, remember, and return to yourself.

Within these pages you will find a series of Explorations, one for each of nine aspects of your being. Each Exploration offers instructions and inquiries to help you design new attitudes, contemplate fresh perspectives, and stay on track with your intentions. You will uncover habitual emotions, thought tendencies, and chosen habits. You will refine your own voice and vision, and recognize what makes your heart happy. You will learn to invite the circumstances, insights, and energetic connections that will help you to be of service to yourself and the world around you.

Every Exploration begins with a meditation, a chance to contemplate from a new vantage point. You will then encounter a series of questions to consider, contemplations to ponder, lists to create, and messages to write to who you were or will be at different stages of your life. Some pages will invite your response to statements like "This is how I give myself love" or "Some part of me knows how to heal this." Some pages give specific instructions and some are more open-ended. Near the end of each Exploration, you'll have a chance to become the author of your own prayers. These prompts might be in the form of a question, an affirmation, or a simple invocation. Meant to move you to give voice to your most unfinished, raw, passing emotions, this journal will help you to refine your listening, elevate your inner dialogue, meet your deepest self with compassion and love, and amplify the inherent intelligence of your own heart.

You might engage the Explorations in order, or you might trust the moment by asking a question and opening to the page that calls to you. Don't be afraid to make a mess or to be precise and clear—be YOU, as you are, every time you write in this journal. When you reflect on your musings, put your attention on the baseline softness beneath it all—the sweet, almost childlike longing to be heard, felt, seen, accepted, and loved for precisely who and where you are. Let these pages spark a sense of reverence for your own path. Let them be a sanctuary in which to gather your perspectives, your priorities, your practices, your purpose, and your prayers.

You are the author of this book; your words make it sacred. Practice You.

"I am here to obey, to obey an authority that I recognize as greater because I am a particle of it. It calls to be recognized, to be served and to shine through me." MADAME JEANNE DE SALZMANN

i am.

embody

BEGIN by taking a moment to sit and get grounded. Place your hands on your thighs, palms down, and begin breathing, deeply and slowly. Breathe audibly at first, then make your breathing increasingly more silent. Sense the weight of your seat, and let your spine rise tall. Feel yourself embodied, present, and steady.

Let the questions on this page serve as continuing contemplations throughout the open spaces to follow. The facing page is left blank for your first responses. Your thoughts will evolve over time, so respect where you are right now, stay steady, and be soft with yourself as you write. If you find yourself filling the page, know that there are more blank pages for additional responses. Keep these questions close as you travel through this Exploration of being and embodiment. You might even return to this initial page now and then to provide yourself with a gentle boundary. As you come to know yourself, you may be surprised to see what's unearthed. Let it out.

- How do you define yourself?

- Who are you today? Can you note some of the "labels" you've placed on yourself, your place in your family, your work, your world?

- What are the words you'd use to describe your current attitude about your life right now?

- What's the most visceral, urgent need you have right now in order to feel alive, happy, and at home in yourself?

- I mostly see myself as an independant & logical. I am loyal & faithful. I think I'm witty, funny, passionate, patient, and so much more.
- Labels: a daughter, sister, crazy (in a fun way), intuitive, sometimes heartless, vital,

- My outlook in life would definitely be optimistic. I am excited to see what is in store for me. I know that God has his plan for me & I'm eager to see what it is.
- I think I need motivation the most

This is who i am when the doubt falls away.

i am

I am at the heart of every observation.

i am all of these things, and none of them.

This is how i love my body.

THIS IS HOW
MY BODY FEELS
after meditation.

This is what i admire most about myself today.

These are the ones who show me who i am.

this is how i commit to an internal experience of love.

THIS is HOW IT FEELS WHEN i BELIEVE IN MYSELF.

THIS is MY prayer To embody
faith in myself.

CONSIDER a moment when you felt challenged, afraid, or sad at age three. See your clothes, your surroundings, your feet. Feel what it would feel like to hug and hold that child. Now, from your perspective and experience today, write a letter, a song, or a poem for that child, sharing a few of the lessons that will be coming in that part of early childhood. Perhaps discuss an influential teacher or best friend. Help that child feel safe, held, and wanted.

i feel.

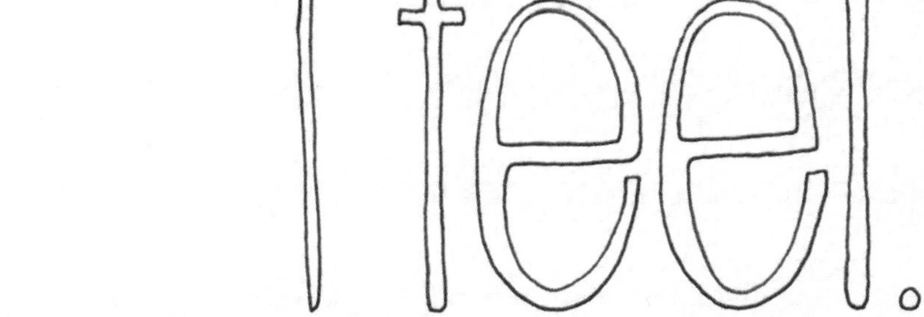

home

BEGIN by taking a moment to let your belly settle. Place your hands on your thighs, palms down, and begin breathing, deeply, slowly, and quietly. Sense the space of your belly opening and receive the gentle wisdom of your emotional body without responding. Just listen for the feelings as they cycle through your being. These sensations are sacred messages of intelligence intended to keep you aware of what needs your attention and bring you back home within yourself.

Let the questions on this page serve as continuing contemplations throughout the open spaces to follow. As before, the facing page is left blank for your first responses. Throughout this Exploration of our primal feelings and how we can make a home for them in our bodies, maintain an awareness of these contemplations with a sense of receptive, sacred awareness. Stay open and be easy with yourself.

- Where and with whom do you feel most at home?
- What does being at home within yourself feel like?
- What feelings need your attention today; what feelings have you been avoiding?
- How can you honor each of those feelings with an act of sweetness?
- Do you believe that you have the capacity to create your experience? If not, why? If so, how?

- I feel most at home when I am alone or with my friends. I, also, feel at home at the beach & I'm in the water
- Feeling at home with yourself feels like

THIS IS WHEN
i FEEL MOST

alive...

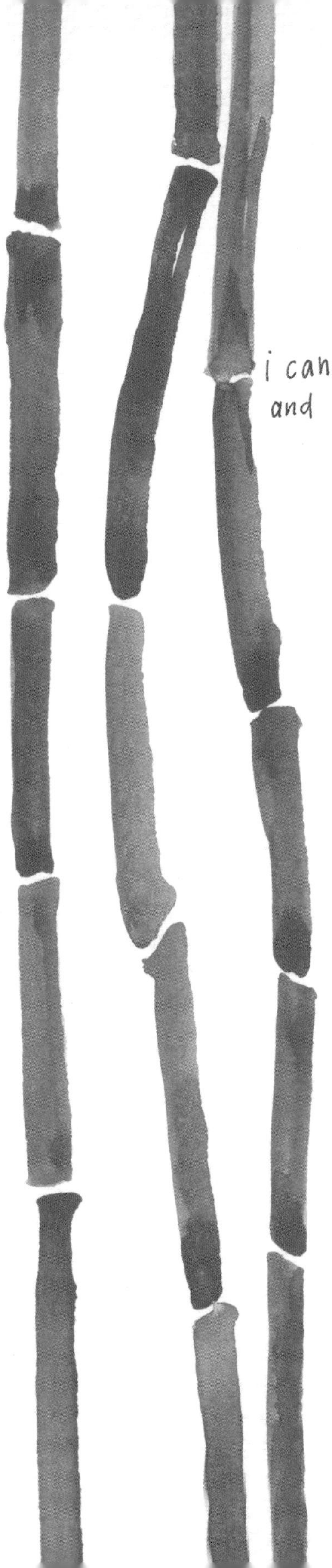

i can bend myself,
and that can help someone else.

These are the emotional states
I have unknowingly invited in.

These are the creative states I am inviting in now.

I choose to be
the Source.

I choose to be
adaptable.

I choose to be
safe.

I choose to be
sweet.

I choose to be.

i choose

this is what i choose to be today.

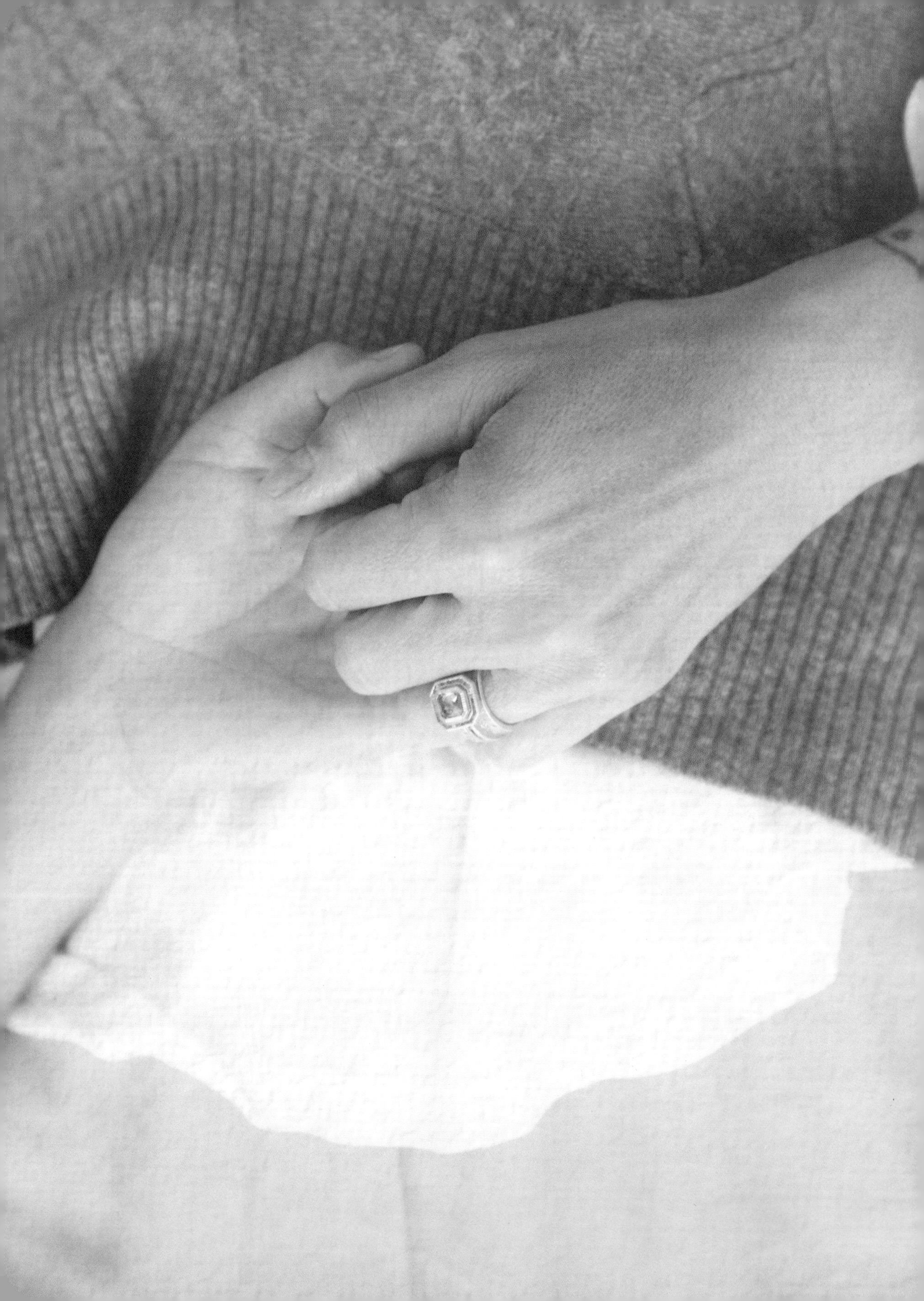

THIS IS WHAT H O M E FEELS LIKE.

This is what my center
feels like.

SILENCE
The universe is listening; think with love.

THIS is
MY Prayer
TO Be aT HoMe
WiTHin MYSeLF.

CONSIDER a moment when you felt challenged, afraid, or sad at age six. From your perspective today, write a song, poem, story, or letter detailing for that child some of the lessons to be learned during this transitional time in middle childhood that will help shape the understandings to come.

ido.

dignity

BEGIN by taking time to sit quietly, hands on your thighs, palms up, arms straight and relaxed, index fingertips and thumbs touching. Let your spine rise tall to create a sensation of regal, receptive readiness. Let your breathing rise and fall naturally, and notice the space just below your heart awakening, feeling energized.

Let the questions on this page serve as continuing contemplations throughout the open spaces to follow. Be vigilant in your observations, but be gentle with yourself. Maintain a sense of dignified presence as you consider these inquiries. When we listen well and offer our attentive awareness to another, a sense of dignity resonates throughout the exchange. In this Exploration of the quality of your actions, listen for the way in which dignity resounds in you.

- How do you define dignity, and how do you bring it to all you do?

- How does outer dignity differ from inner dignity?

- How do you bestow dignity upon yourself?

- How do you bestow dignity on those closest to you?

This is how I
respect
myself.
These are my
practices.

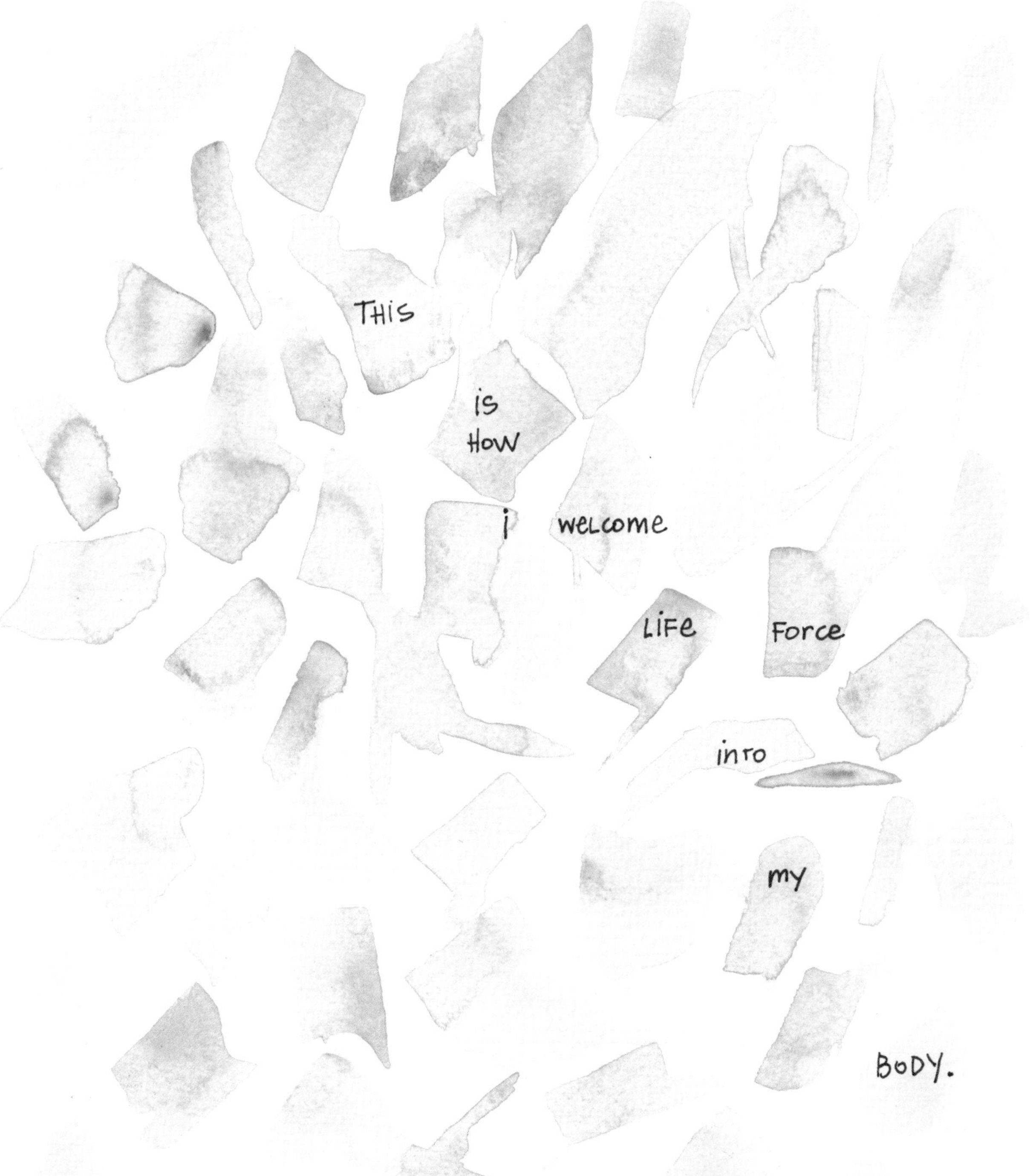
THIS
is
HOW
i
welcome
LIFE
Force
into
my
BODY.

this is who i am when i am in my power,
when i am cultivating my soul-force.

this is what i do daily
to feel whole and awake:

- [ ] meditate. i listen to my breathing. i lengthen it.
i lose track. i come back.

- [ ] pray. i look to my guides. i ask. i receive.

- [ ] create. i sit with all the colors.
i surrender. i begin.

these are the blessings i offer

to the MOTHERS and the FATHERS

this is how i restore harmony:

i begin with forgiveness...

i land in compassion.

this is how i

pray for softness.

how can discipline be a surrender

to the *feminine*?

THese are My Daily prayers Going up.

CONSIDER a moment when you felt challenged, afraid, or sad at age nine. See yourself hugging that child you were. Now, from your perspective today, write a song, poem, letter, or story that gives that child insight into the ways you will soon learn to know yourself, to believe in yourself, and to bestow dignity upon yourself by trusting yourself.

i love.

love

BEGIN by taking time to sit quietly, hands on your thighs, palms up, arms straight and relaxed, tips of your ring fingers touching your thumbs. Let your spine rise tall and breathe into the space of love in the center of your heart. Let your breathing rise and fall naturally, and let that love lift and be amplified.

Let the questions on this page serve as continuing contemplations throughout the open spaces to follow. Stay loving and present for yourself. Throughout this Exploration, hold the light of this love in your heart. Nourish yourself with your writings.

- When have you felt truly loved and cared for, whether by yourself or by another?
- Where does that love live in your body?
- What thoughts arise from the sensation of love?
- How could you be more available to receive love? To give love?

THIS is HOW i GIVE MYSELF L O V E.

THIS is HOW
i PRACTICE
inner dignity.

MY LOVE is
PATIENT.
MY PATIENCE
is LOVE.

inner dignity feels like this.

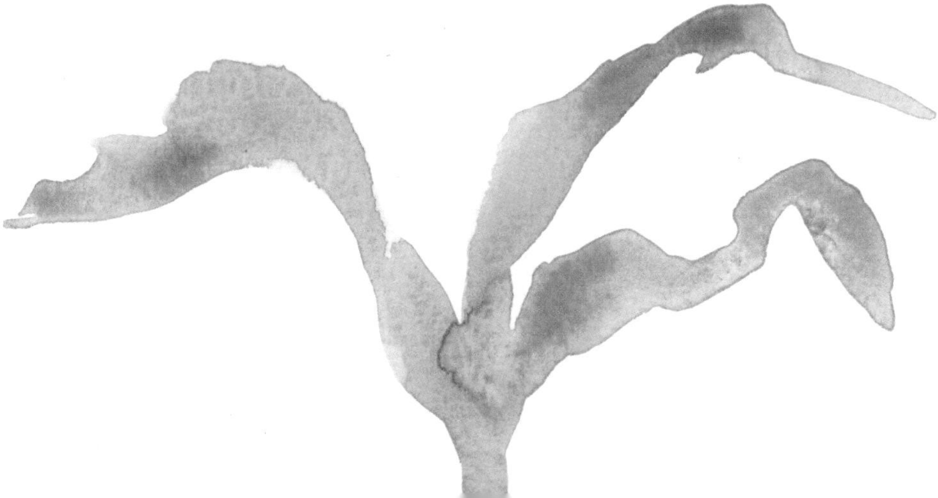

i am clear in my love. i radiate love. i act from love. i grow my love.

i respect love. I take time for love.

i find new reasons and ways to express love.

....this is how i let love out.

this is how i let love in...

THIS is How i
STay in my
Heart.

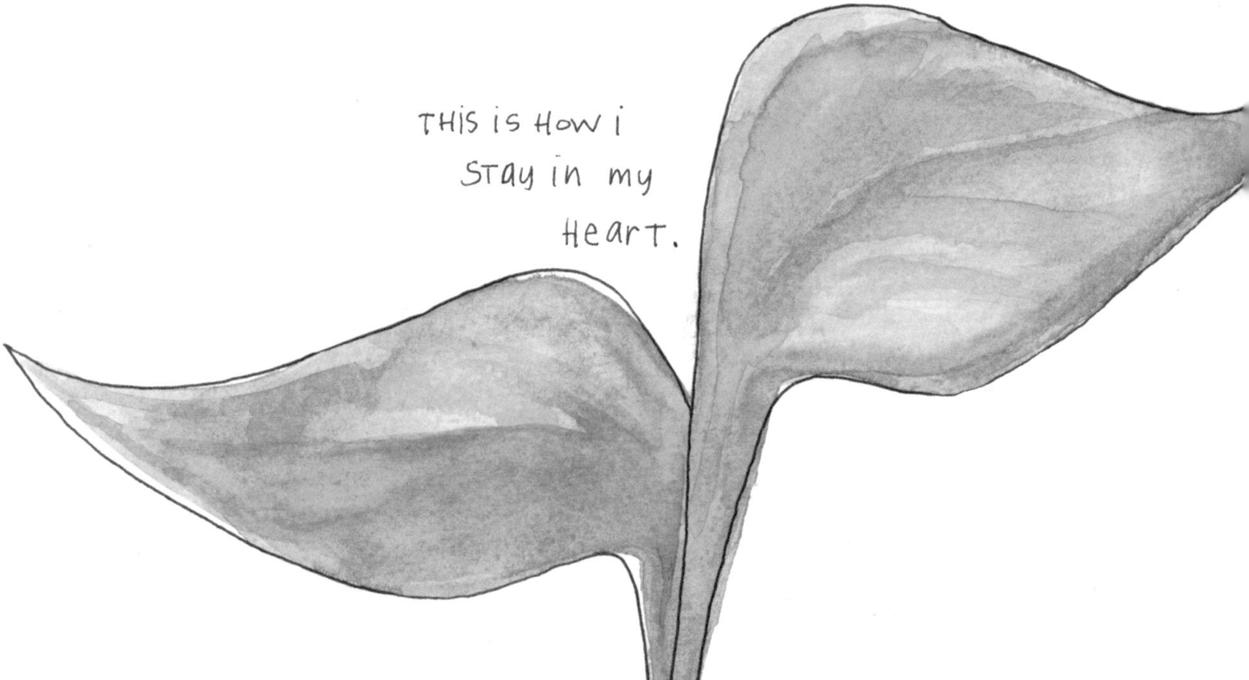

this is how i give direction to my love.

How have my heartbreaks helped me find my tribe?

THESE ARE THE PEOPLE I'VE CHOSEN, WHO'VE ALSO CHOSEN ME.

THIS IS MY SOUL

FAMILY TREE.

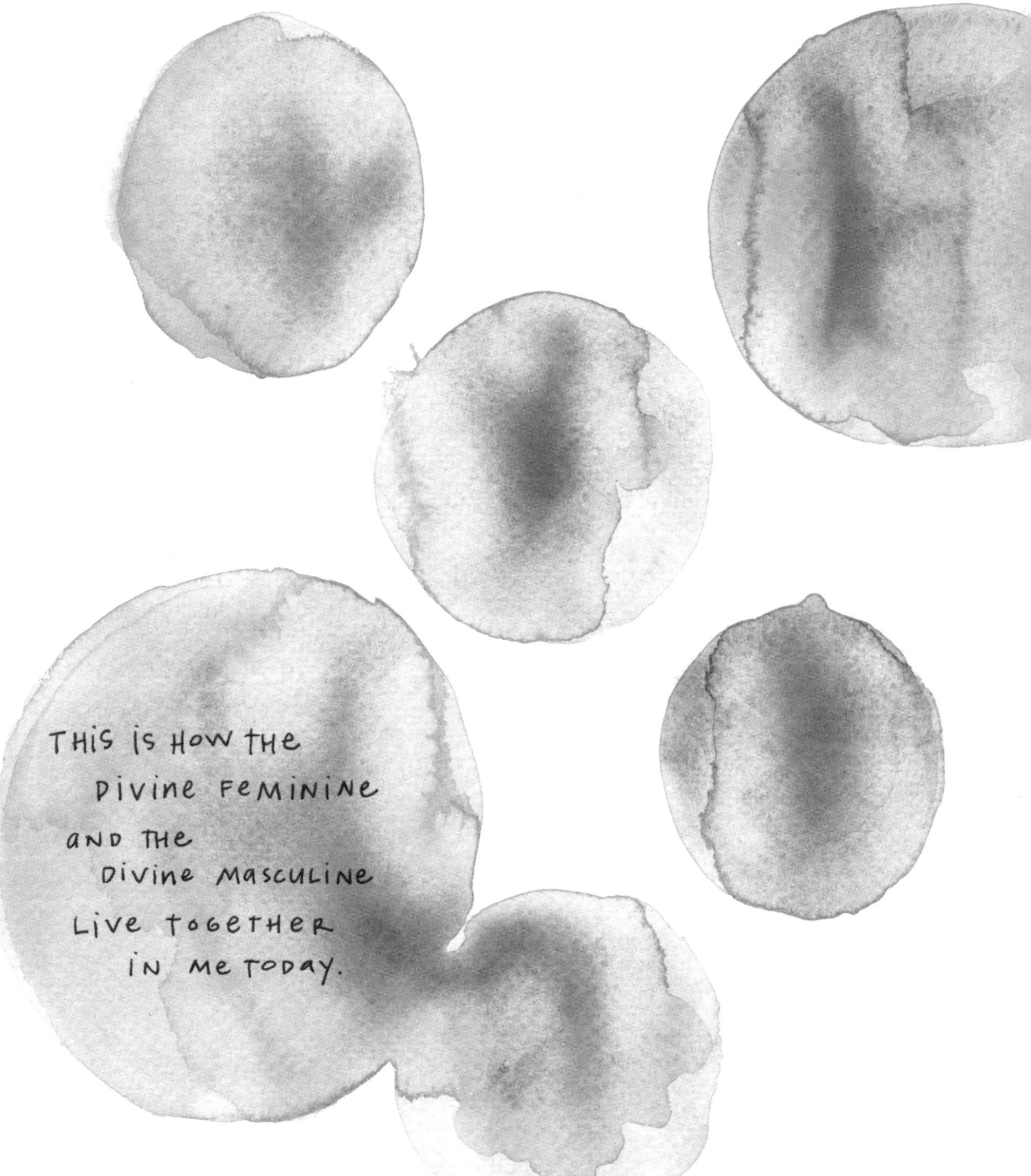
THIS IS HOW THE
DIVINE FEMININE
AND THE
DIVINE MASCULINE
LIVE TOGETHER
IN ME TODAY.

These are my thoughts of compassion for myself.

this is my blessing of Love.

this blessing has no beginning and no end.

CONSIDER a moment when you felt challenged, afraid, or sad at age 12. See yourself sitting near and helping yourself at that age to feel safe and seen. From your perspective today, detail the most influential understandings to be gained in the coming early teen years in a letter, poem, song, or story.

i speak.

listen

SIT QUIETLY, hands on your thighs, palms up, arms straight and relaxed, tips of your pinkies touching your thumbs. Let your spine rise tall, and breathe into your upper chest and throat. Let your breathing come in and out naturally, and open your faculties of listening.

Let the questions on this page serve as continuing contemplations throughout the open spaces to follow. In this Exploration of the quality of your speech, listen to the words that arise in your mind as you read through the inquiries. Capture them. Stay connected to the quality of your thoughts, as well as the quality of the silence within you. That silence is the ground of knowing and speaking your truth, granting forgiveness where it's most needed, and loving yourself with the words you use internally.

- Choose five words you would use to describe yourself today.

- Name someone you know who's a great listener. What do they do when they're listening to you?

- How does it feel to be truly heard?

- Is there anyone in your world to whom you could apologize today? Make a note (no need to send it unless you wish; just noting).

- What does forgiveness mean to you?

- Is there anyone in your life you could forgive today?

THIS is WHaT i aM aFraiD TO SAY.

BUT i KNOW iT WiLL SeT Me Free TO SAY iT.

THIS is How silence feels.

...how i talk to myself...

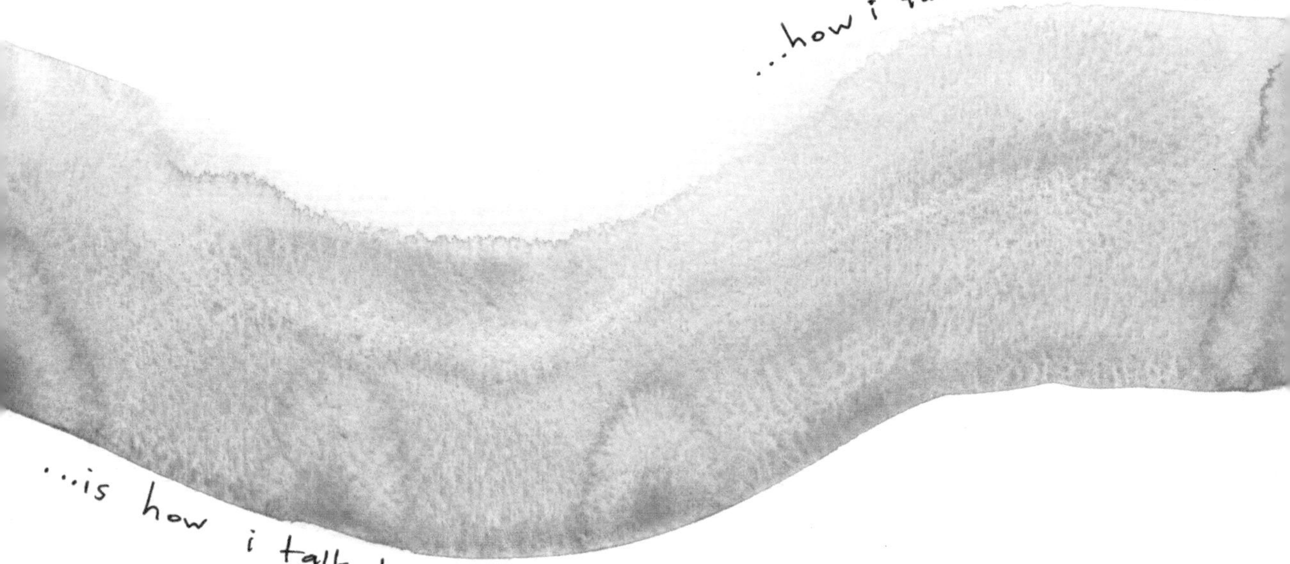

...is how i talk to others...

these are the people
to whom i could listen more attentively.

this is how
FORGIVENESS begins.

This is how I become like water.

this is how i love myself with my words.

"What we speak becomes the house we live in." - Hafiz
These are the words with which i choose to
B U i L D.

Have no agenda.

Listen respectfully.

Mother yourself.

Be a loving listener.

Trust your intuition.

Be comfortable with silence.

CHOOSE A TEACHING FROM THE FACING PAGE THAT SPEAKS TO YOU.

WRITE THE STEPS TO MAKE IT SO.

These are the blessings that are touching me today.

CONSIDER who you were, or who you might be, at age 15. What are you wearing? How are you feeling? Who is closest to you? From your perspective today, write a letter, poem, story, or song detailing the sacred lessons to be learned between the ages of 15 and 18. If you're younger than 15, write a piece on who you dream of becoming.

i see.

insight

SIT QUIETLY, hands on your thighs, palms up, arms straight and relaxed, fingers open. Let your spine rise tall, and breathe into the center of your brain. Let your breathing rise and fall naturally, and widen your eyes. Broaden your brow. Notice a small smile forming in your eyes and mouth.

Let the questions on this page serve as continuing contemplations throughout the open spaces and pages to follow. Throughout these inquiries, maintain a connection to what you see and hear in your mind, and practice allowing the perceptions to dissolve readily. Be open to new possibilities and ideas. Listen well as you write, so new pathways can reveal themselves.

- Name one insight you've recently realized that has helped you move forward.
- What are you now seeing that you weren't seeing even a few months or weeks ago?
- How has that shifted your ways of seeing anything and anyone in your life?

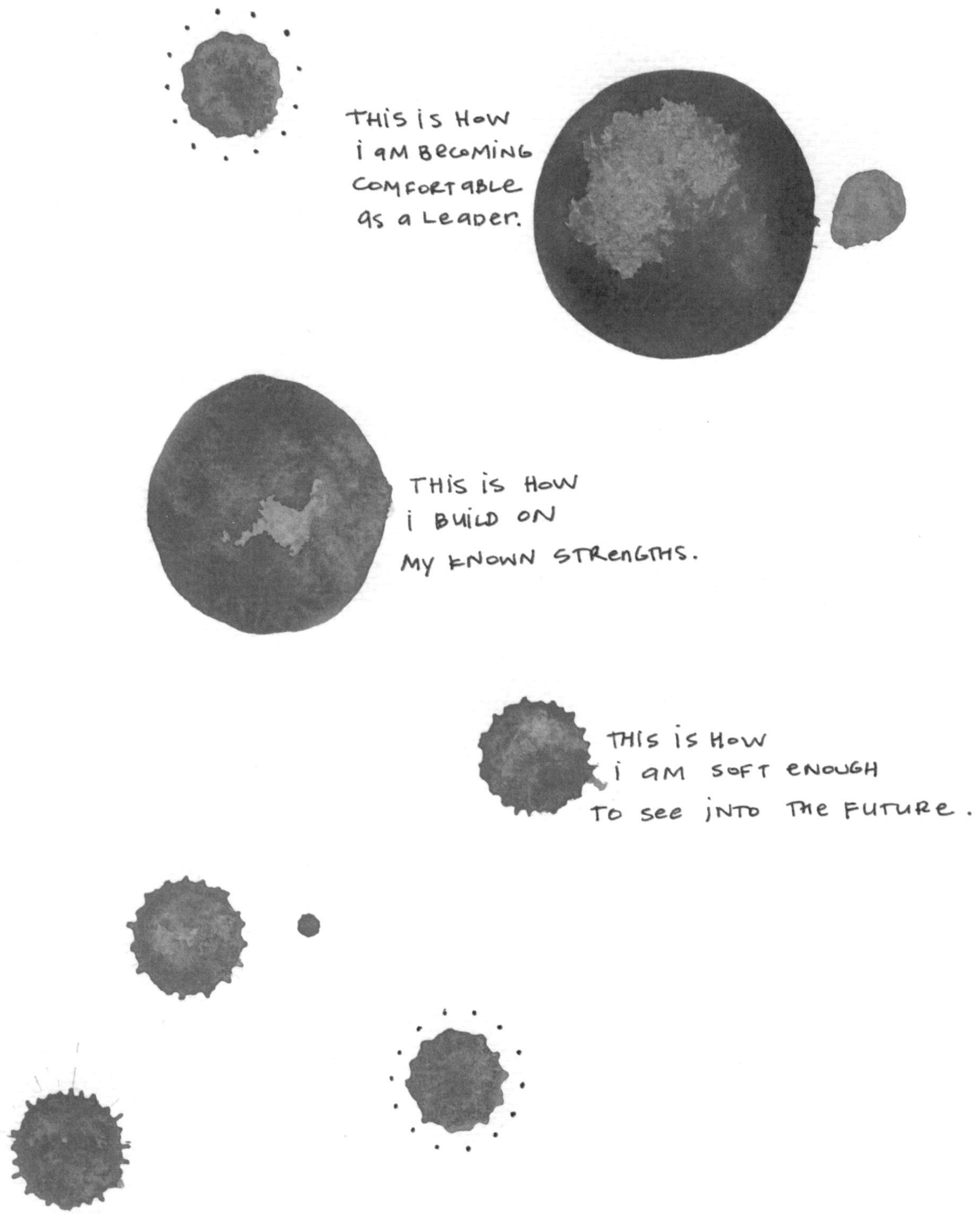
THIS IS HOW
I AM BECOMING
COMFORTABLE
AS A LEADER.
THIS IS HOW
I BUILD ON
MY KNOWN STRENGTHS.
THIS IS HOW
I AM SOFT ENOUGH
TO SEE INTO THE FUTURE.

THIS IS MY VISION FOR HOW I LEAD. . . .

LONGING
BELONGING

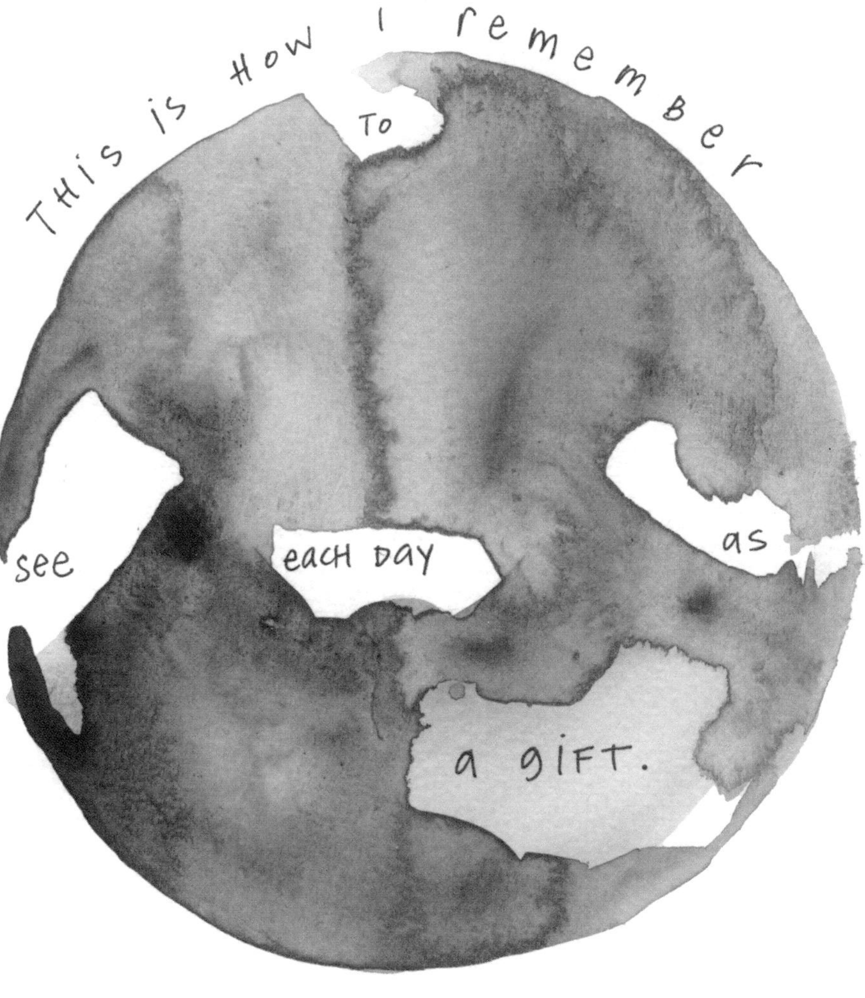
THIS is How i remember
To
see
each Day
as
a gift.

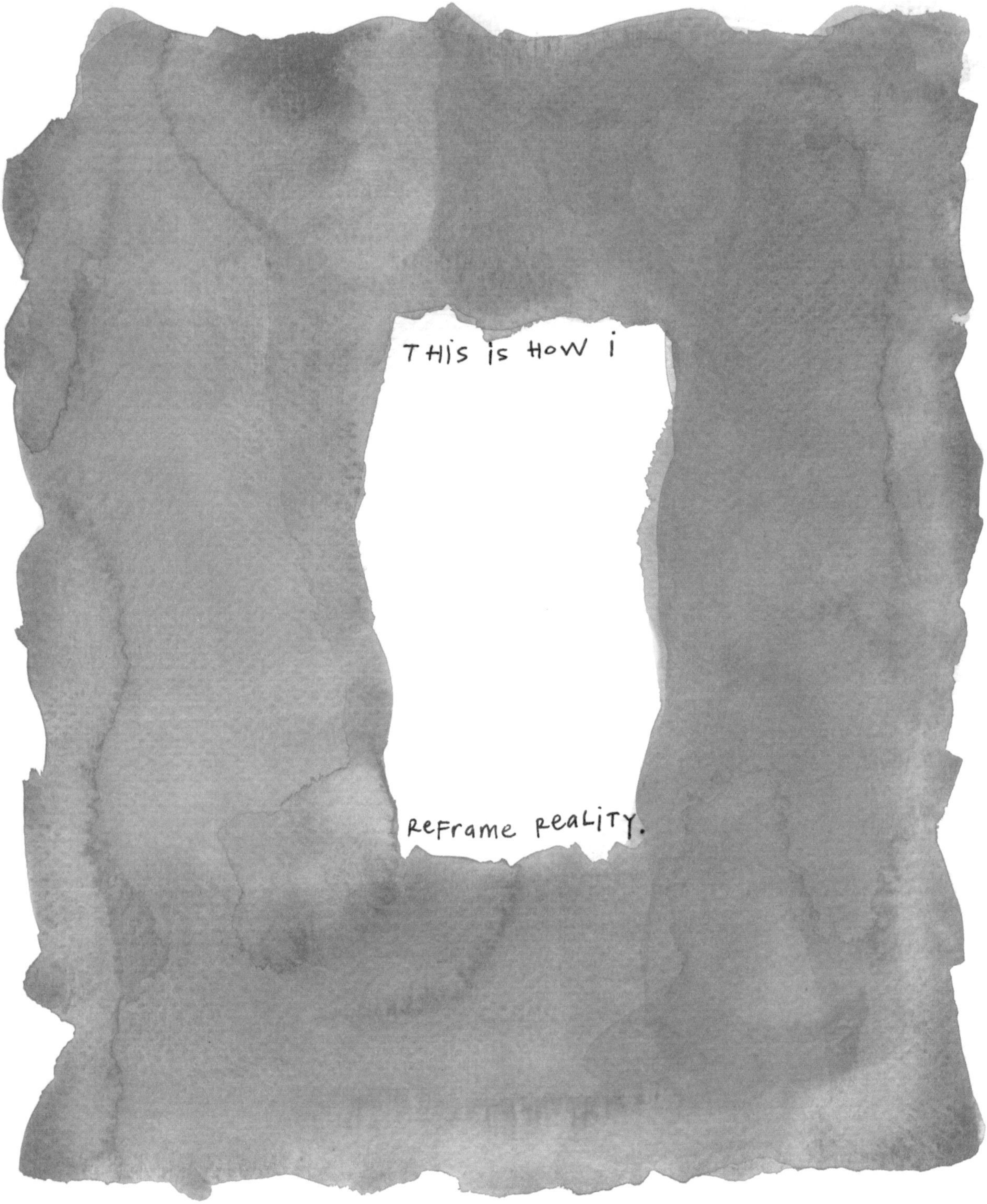
THIS is HOW i
reframe reaLiTY.

THIS IS HOW MY SIMPLEST SHIFT IN PERCEPTION

GRANTS PROFOUND HEALING.

Always be bigger
and more compassionate
than you think you can be.

Stay close to
yourself when
it hurts.

Ask more questions.
Speak less than ever.

Love yourself.

Make
space.

Consider what you're
about to say
at least twice.

Keep your word.

Go easy on
yourself.

Develop knowledge of your
own.

Realize you're asleep
and you're already half awake.

when i soften my
eyes, this is what i
see in my heart.

THIS IS WHAT I'M releasing.
THIS IS WHAT I'M AMPLIFYING.

THIS is MY prayer FOR

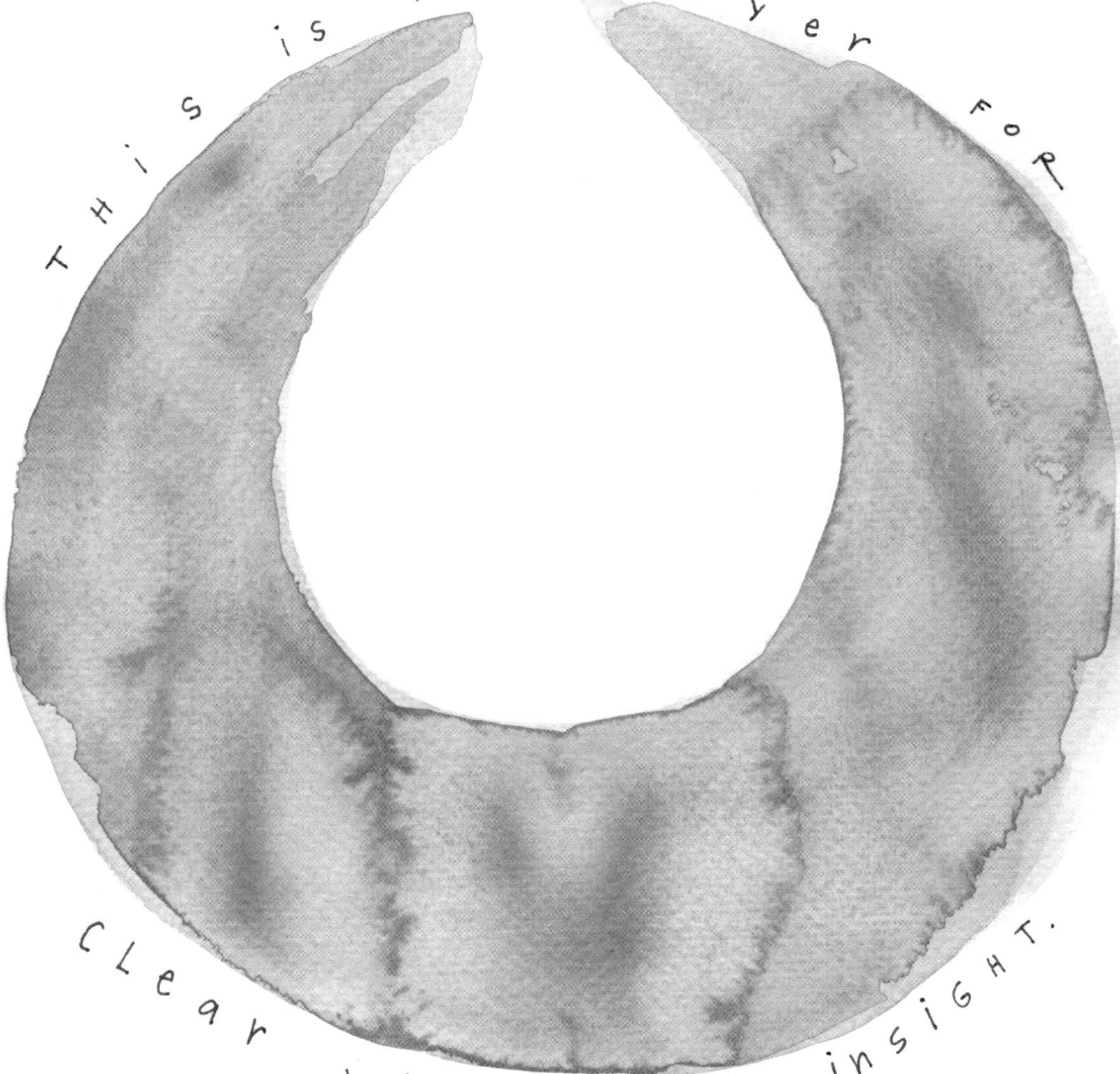

Clear Vision and insiGHT.

CONSIDER yourself at age 21. If you are not yet 21, write a letter, poem, story, or song detailing all the things you wish you could learn from your future self. If you are older than 21, write a letter, poem, story, or song about one wondrous, momentous occasion that has occurred in the years since you were that age. Through the lens of your current wisdom and experience, offer your 21-year-old self one note about how to take care of your body and one about how to take care of your mind.

i understand.

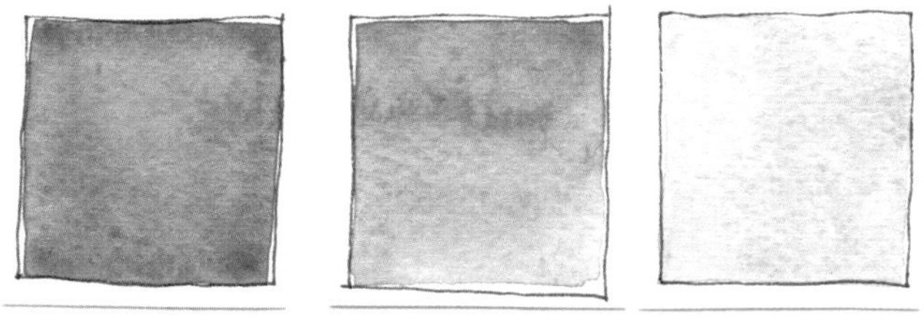

wisdom

SIT QUIETLY, hands on your thighs, palms up, arms straight and relaxed, index fingers and thumbs touching. Let your spine rise tall, and breathe into your crown, at the very top of your head. Breathe naturally and feel a sense of uplift from your heart upward, as though you are being elevated vertically from within, yet remaining grounded.

Let the questions on this page serve as continuing contemplations throughout the open spaces to follow. Wisdom can be considered a state in which you are connected to Spirit, to Source, to your own highest knowing. In this Exploration of your connection to truth, be receptive to the most cosmic, divine possibilities landing in your life. Let yourself write them down.

- When do you feel most connected to Spirit, to Source?
- When do you sense you are at your most awake and aware of yourself as a divine being?
- In what context and with whom do you feel most at home, most yourself?
- What is the difference between your outer life and your inner life?

THIS is HOW
MY OUTER WORLD
REFLECTS
MY inner LIFE.

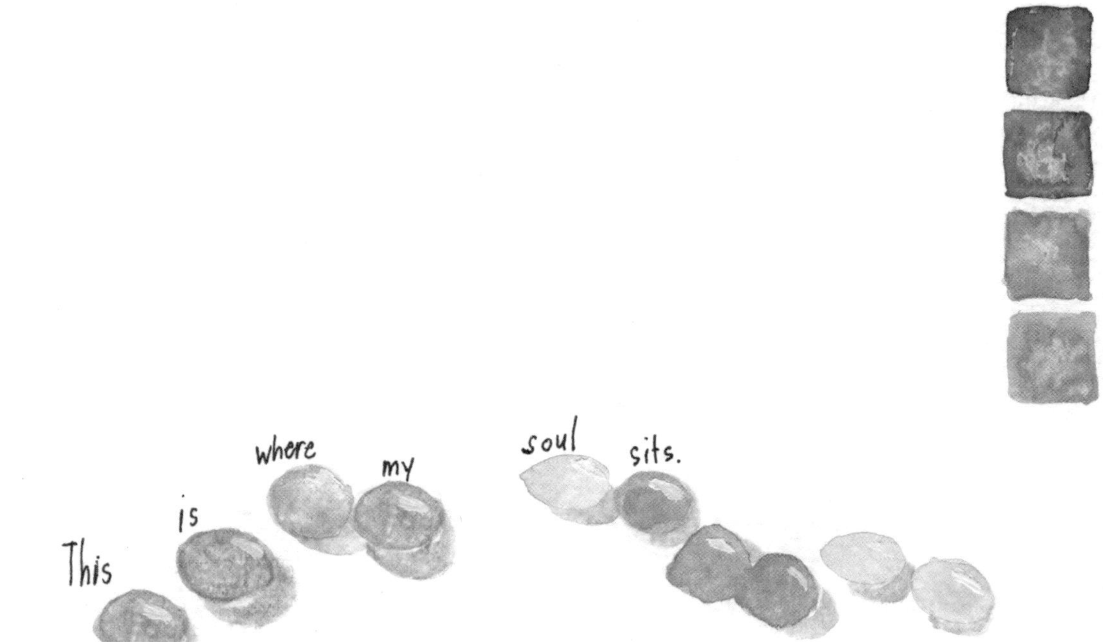
This is where my soul sits.

These are the habits I'm creating

To become my highest self.

home

is not a place. home is a state of consciousness.
home is my forgiveness. home is my alchemy.
home is my promise. home is my empathy.
home is my humanity. and yes, home is my family,
with their crazy and their beauty.
and home is the creation i fashion from reality;
home is even the illusion of separation from my highest identity;
home is the place where i get to be evolutionary.
home is touching, greeting, recognizing, embracing;
home is seeing into the depths of someone else's true nature.
home is exploring, accepting, and liberating.
home is oneness, it's guidance, it's listening, it's stunning.
TODAY, i GIVE THANKS FOR THIS INVITATION,
this investigation, THIS HOMECOMING.

this is how **worry** becomes **wisdom**.

THis is HoW i practice LuMiNous FreeDoM.

THIS is HOW i TRANSFORM BLAME into Bravery.

THIS IS HOW I EVOLVE WITH REVERENCE.

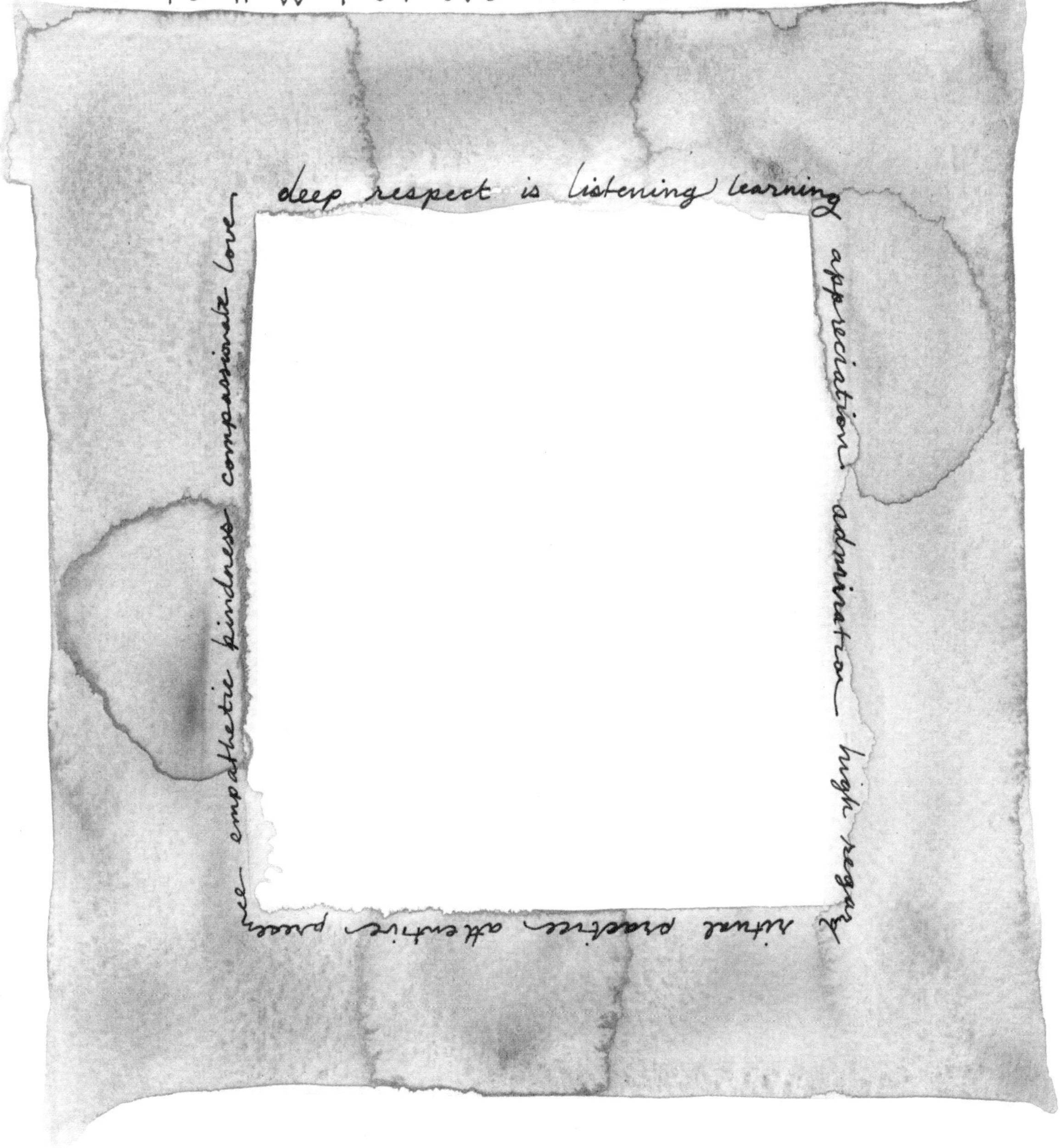

this is how
i put the pieces
back together
after i've torn
myself apart.

There is nobody to blame
nothing to fear
nowhere to hide
no secret to keep.
There is

one love

one heart
one light
one body
one privilege
one source
one family.

THIS IS MY prayer FOR evOLUTION.

CONSIDER your 33-year-old self. If you are not yet 33, take a moment to connect to who you will be at that age. Write a letter, poem, story, or song from that 33-year-old perspective to the person you are now. What does home feel like to that future you? How have you come home to yourself in the years between now and age 33? If you're past the age of 33, write a message to yourself at that age detailing your highest understanding of what "home" feels like from your current perspective. What does your previous self have to look forward to when it comes to creating a sensation of home?

i trust.

integrity

SIT QUIETLY, left hand to your heart. Let your spine rise tall, and sense the circumference of your body receiving your breathing. Feel a sense of breathing beyond the periphery of your own body, as though you can grow into the space around you.

Let these questions serve as continuing contemplations throughout the open spaces to follow. Consider your relationship to, and definition of, integrity. Integrity is the state in which the heart, mind, and body are all aimed in the same direction, toward the same goal. In this Exploration of the relationship between trust and integrity, allow yourself the safety to be honest with yourself. Be gentle and fearless with yourself.

- What does trust mean to you?

- In what ways and contexts are you trustworthy? Untrustworthy?

- Name a time when you were dishonest with yourself, or with others.

- Think of someone you trust completely. How have they earned your trust?

- Name a circumstance or two when you have seen integrity in action. How did that inspire you?

Some part of me knows how to heal this.

i am standing on sacred ground.

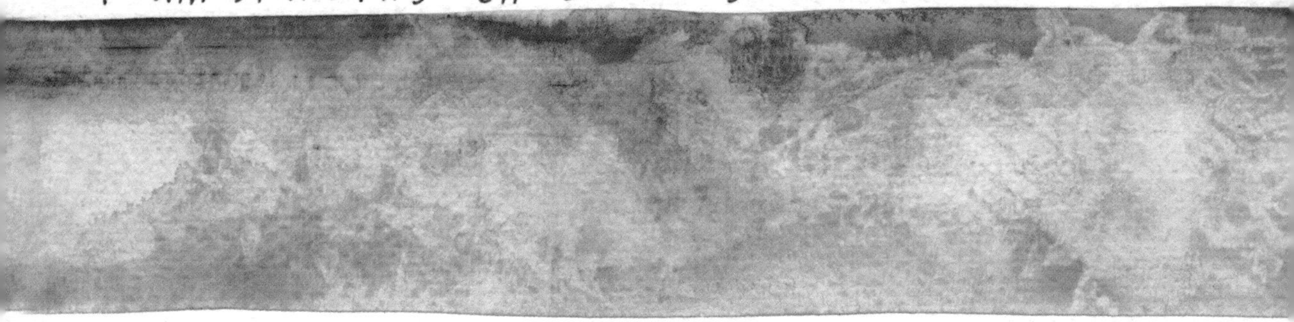

THIS IS WHAT I TRUST RIGHT NOW.

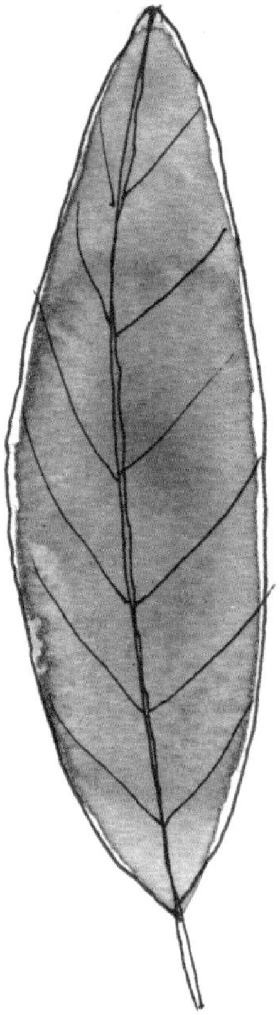

"The reality is there is nobody who can limit you. There is nobody who can damage you. Your existence is not bound in time and space. You always have a choice of how you project your mind."

Yogi Bhajan

THIS IS MY REMINDER TO MYSELF.

i am held. i am safe. i am free. i am wise.

i am ______________________________

THIS is WHAT MOVES ME TOWARD MEANING.

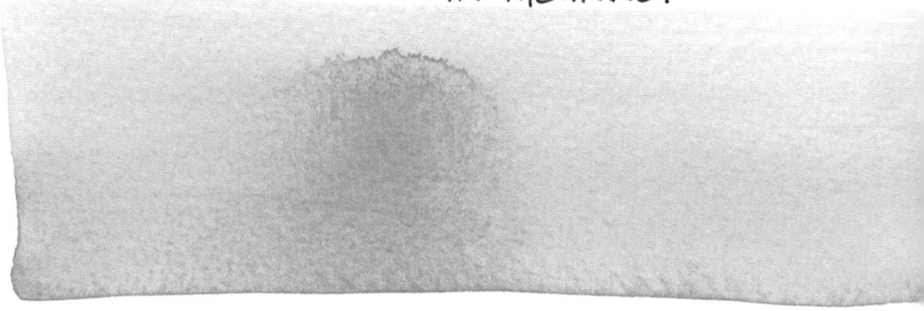

THIS IS WHO I'M BECOMING.

Sometimes i FLY; i LET GO,
i GO HIGH. IT FEELS LIKE
T H I S

This is how i

let

go

when it's time.

THIS IS HOW I LIVE WITH AMBIGUITY, CONSISTENTLY,

THIS IS HOW I ATTUNE TO HUMILITY. . . .

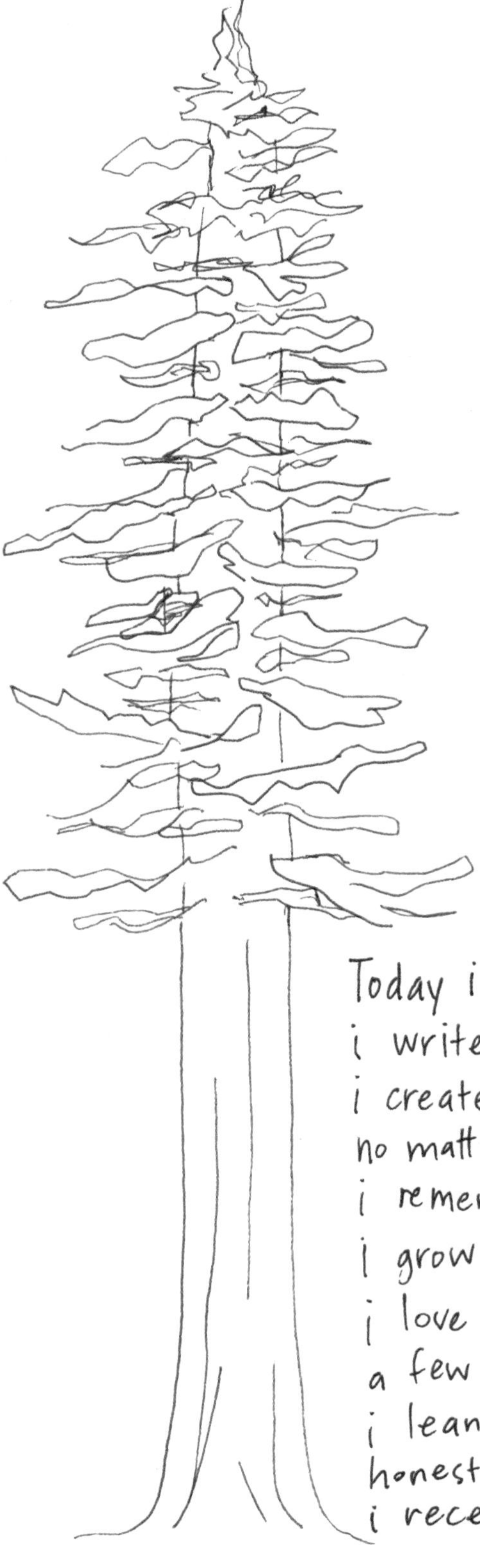

Today i tell the truth.
i write a little.
i create one piece of art,
no matter how small.
i remember myself at least once.
i grow my spine tall.
i love myself inside and out,
a few moments at a time.
i lean on the Universe with my
honesty. i ask for signs.
i receive them gratefully.

THIS is MY prayer TO stay CONSCIOUS WHEN i FORGET TO TRUST.

CONSIDER your 55-year-old self. If you are not yet 55, take a moment to connect to who you will be at that age. Write a letter, story, poem, or song to who you are now from that 55-year-old's perspective, detailing what you have learned about integrity and trustworthiness over the course of your life. If you're past the age of 55, write a message to yourself detailing your highest understanding of integrity from your current perspective. What does your 55-year-old self need to know about trust and truth-telling?

i serve.

freedom

SIT QUIETLY, both hands resting on your heart. Let your spine rise tall, breathing deeply, listening for your own inner guidance.

As you make notes in the spaces that follow, maintain a connection to yourself and to your freedom. In this final Exploration, contemplate the relationship between your greatest offering and your ultimate liberation.

- How does your presence communicate your essence?

- What does service mean to you?

- How and whom do you serve presently? Please include your household, children, parents, friends, pets.

- How do you serve yourself?

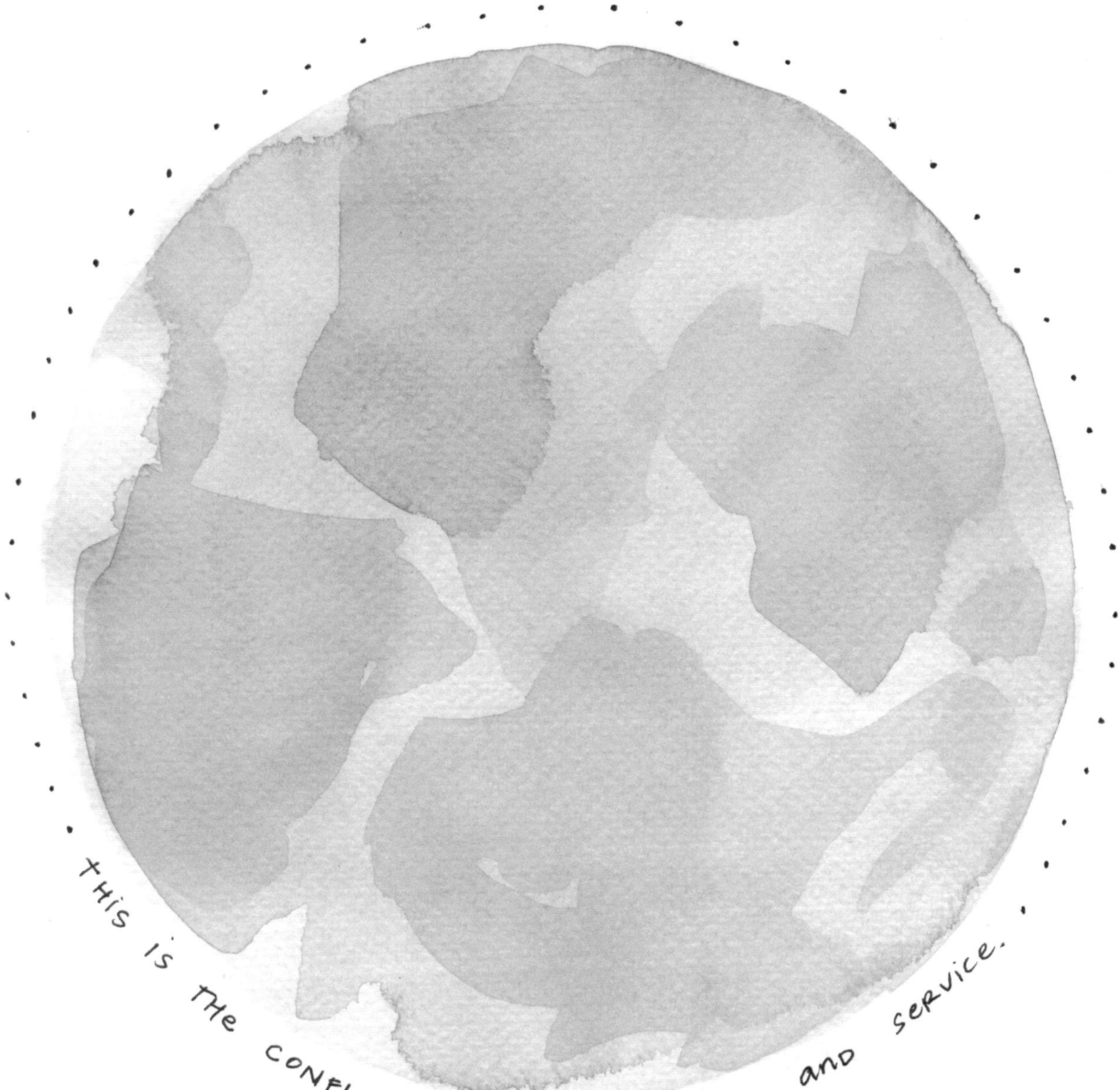
this is the confluence of self-care and service.

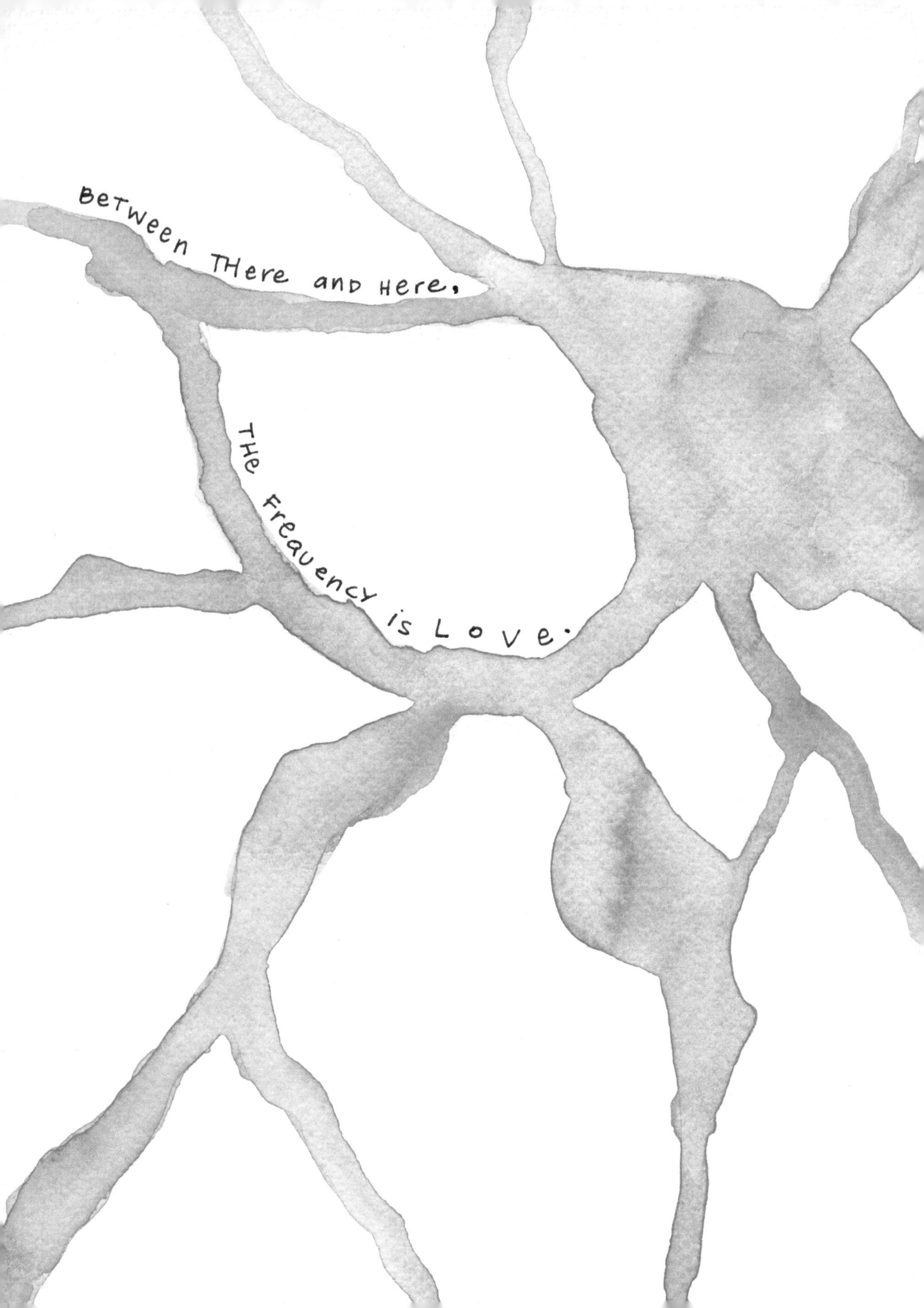
Between There and Here,
The Frequency is Love.

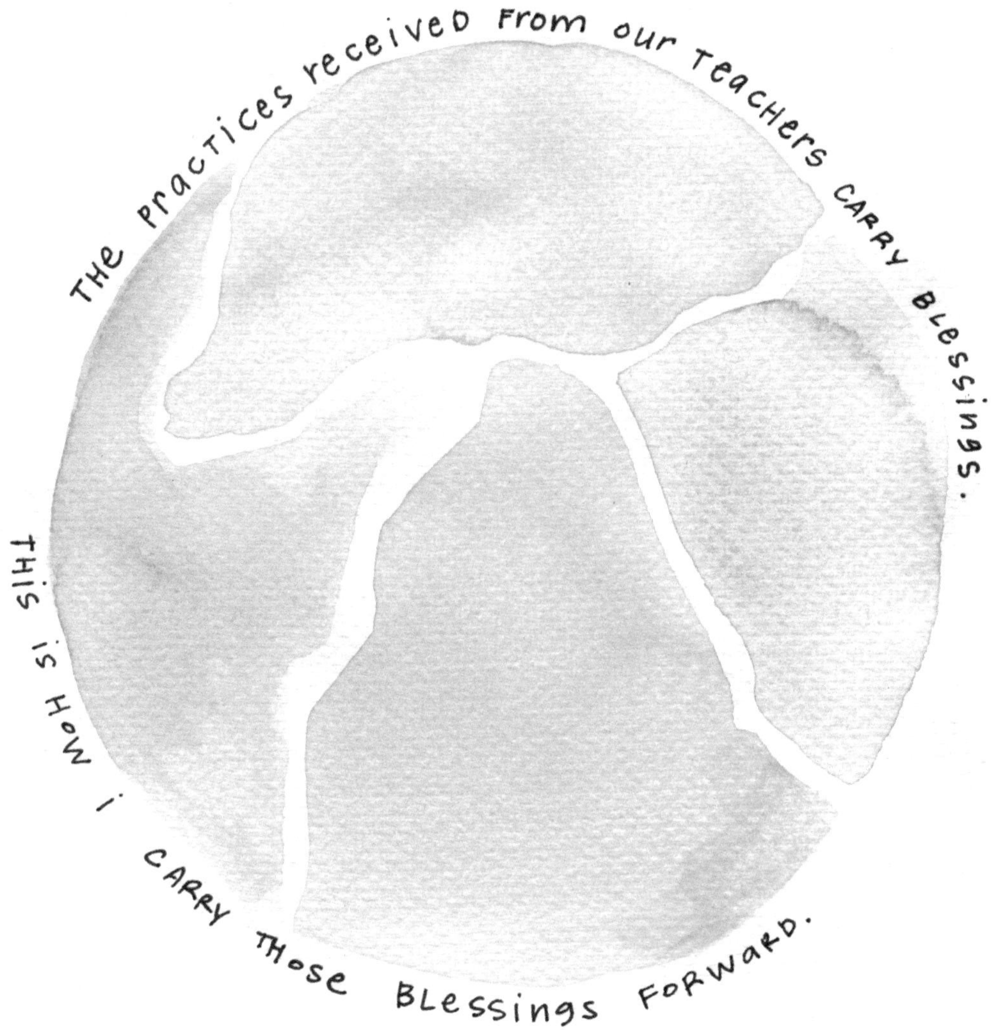
THE practices received from our Teachers CARRY BLessings.
THIS is How i CARRY THose BLessings FORWARD.

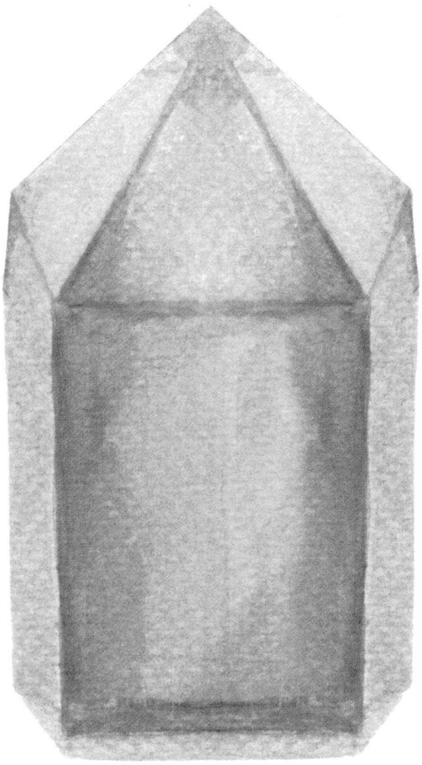

THIS is HOW i serve WITH TenDerness.

THIS is THE innermost Temple.

this is where i remain unshaken in my

SOUL.

this is what i'm

serving

right now.

THIS is HOW i HOLD SPACE.

"My whole effort, my whole work... is to maintain a body
so relaxed that the energy does not leave."

Madame Jeanne de Salzmann

this is how i further evolution in my family.

We are related to each other.
By taking care of myself, I take care of you.
By taking care of you, I take care of myself.
This is my prayer for knowing how to help.

CONSIDER your 99-year-old self. Take a moment to connect with that future you. Write a letter, poem, story, or song to yourself now from that century-long perspective. At that age, what is your conception of presence as it relates to your highest service in this life? What does serving yourself and others have to do with freedom? What is the most important message that future self has for who you are now?

acknowledgments

Mama, thank you for never leaving my side, for filling my heart with trust in your presence, and for continuously and conspicuously reminding me of who I am.

Jones, my light and my teacher, thank you for being patient while I painted and worked on this project.

Daddy, Jess, Jeff, Cory, Jenny, and Henry, for making me laugh and keeping me close. Anthony and Gabrielle, for your steadfast love and trust.

James Benard, thank you for your eyes, your heart, your love, your partnership.

Kevin Sullivan, for the care with which you've ushered this book to life.

Jennifer Murray, for organizing, arranging, and catalyzing my heart to create.

Lynn Hazan, my business partner, for every bit of all of it.

Michelle Martello and Zane Gibbs, for the visioning sessions and your kindness.

Ewa de Cruz, for the feathers of evolution and ascension.

Sidney Bensimon, for your photographs, and your listening.

My teachers, Yogarupa Rod Stryker, Hari Kaur Khalsa, Nevine Michaan, Abbie Galvin, Paramatma Siri Sadhana, Shiva Rea: I'm here because you are.

My women, my witches: your presence gives me glimpses of true grace.

And my business tribe, my team: bless you for your attention and care.

My art teachers, Joan Hochberg, Pedro Cano, and Mary Ellen Bonifati McGeough: thank you for being the true beginning of this book, and for enriching my school years.

And thank you to the Sounds True team, for your care, your trust, and your vision:

Brian Galvin
Jennifer Y. Brown
Karen Polaski
Rachael Murray
Leslie Brown
Wendy Pardo
Andrew Young
Kira Roark
Wendy Gardner

about the author

Elena Brower has been teaching yoga since 1998. She is also a visual artist, writer, and designer. Her book *Art of Attention* has been translated into six languages. Elena is the founder of Teach.yoga, a virtual home for teachers in over sixty countries worldwide. Learn more at practiceyou.com.

about Sounds True

Sounds True is a multimedia publisher whose mission is to inspire and support personal transformation and spiritual awakening. Founded in 1985 and located in Boulder, Colorado, we work with many of the leading spiritual teachers, thinkers, healers, and visionary artists of our time. We strive with every title to preserve the essential "living wisdom" of the author or artist. It is our goal to create products that not only provide information to a reader or listener, but that also embody the quality of a wisdom transmission.

For those seeking genuine transformation, Sounds True is your trusted partner. At SoundsTrue.com you will find a wealth of free resources to support your journey, including exclusive weekly audio interviews, free downloads, interactive learning tools, and other special savings on all our titles.

To learn more, please visit SoundsTrue.com/freegifts or call us toll-free at 800.333.9185.

SOUNDS TRUE
many voices, one journey

Sounds True, Inc.

Boulder, CO 80306

This work is solely for personal growth and education. It should not be treated as a substitute for professional assistance, therapeutic activities such as psychotherapy or counseling, or medical advice. In the event of physical or mental distress, please consult with appropriate health professionals. The application of protocols and information in this book is the choice of each reader, who assumes full responsibility for his or her understandings, interpretations, and results. The author and publisher assume no responsibility for the actions or choices of any reader.

Cover and book design by Rachael Murray

Art by Elena Brower

Photography by Sidney Bensimon

Printed in South Korea

Library of Congress Control Number: 2017905963

ISBN: 978-1-62203-922-7

10 9 8 7 6 5